GREAT PETS
Freshwater Fishes

Marjorie L. Buckmaster

Marshall Cavendish
Benchmark
New York

Marshall Cavendish Benchmark
99 White Plains Road
Tarrytown, New York 10591-9001
www.marshallcavendish.us

Library of Congress Cataloging-in-Publication Data

Buckmaster, Marjorie L.
Freshwater fishes / by Marjorie L. Buckmaster.
p. cm. -- (Great pets)
Summary: "Describes the characteristics and behavior of freshwater fishes
kept as pets, also discussing the physical appearance and place in the
history of these fishes"--Provided by publisher.
Includes index.
ISBN 978-0-7614-2712-4
1. Aquarium fishes--Juvenile literature. I. Title.
SF457.25.B83 2007
639.34--dc22
                                        2007017809

Photo research by Candlepants, Inc.
Front cover credit: age fotostock / Super Stock
The photographs in this book are used by permission and through the courtesy of: Minden Pictures: Wil
Meinderts/Foto Natura, 1, 27. Corbis: Christie's Images, 4; Claro Cortes IV/Reuters, 14; Jörg Carstensen/dpa, 30; DK
Limited, 32. Art Resource,NY: HIP, 6. Photo Researchers Inc.: John Sanford & David Parker, 7; Mark Smith, 12, 14, 15;
David Schleser / Nature's Images, 21; Doug Martin, 42; Gregory K. Scott, 45; The Bridgeman Art Library: ©Roy Miles
Fine Paintings, 8. Peter Arnold Inc.: PHONE Labat J.M. / Rouquette, 10, 18, 24, 28; PHONE Labat Jean-Michel, 37;
BIOS Cavignaux Bruno, back cover. ShutterStock: Feng Yu, 13; Eric Issellee, 22; Stuart Elflett, 35. Super Stock:
SuperStock Inc. 20. Getty Images: Rob Goldman, 34; David E Perry, 38. Jupiter Images: Stewart Charles Cowen, 41.

Editor: Karen Ang
Publisher: Michelle Bisson
Art Director: Anahid Hamparian
Series Designer: Elynn Cohen

Printed in Malaysia
6 5 4 3 2 1

Contents

1

Fish Tales

People have been sharing myths or folk stories about fishes for thousands of years and in dozens of languages. Keeping fish as pets is a very old hobby. In China, the goldfish is a symbol of good luck, good fortune, beauty, and harmony. Other countries also see the **carp** as a symbol of good luck and long life. Even seeing a carp in a dream is said to be a sign of good luck. Different types of fishes are also seen as symbols of intelligence, courage, and strength. This might be because many fishes are able to swim against the strong currents of a river.

Fishes play a key part in many myths and religious stories. For example, one popular myth from India tells the story of a man named Manu and how he survived a great flood. Manu had been kind to a fish that later warned him about the deadly flood. Following the fish's advice, Manu built a boat that helped him survive the flood. The fish in that story is supposed

An old Chinese painting shows a carp that was kept as a pet.

This stone structure displays the Indian myth of how a god—disguised as a fish—helped save mankind.

to represent an Indian god. In other myths, the people who ride fishes are messengers of the gods.

Fishes can also be found in the stars. Pisces (which is Latin for "fish") is a constellation, or collection of stars, in the sky. Pisces is also a zodiac sign that is represented by two fish tied together. People who are born between February 19 and March 20 are Pisces.

Fish as Pets

Fish keeping began more than 4,500 years ago. Goldfish (also known as the Asiatic Golden Carp) were originally used as food until about the year 1000, when they became popular as pets in China.

Based on the constellation, the symbol for the Pisces zodiac sign is two fish hooked together.

Throughout history, people from other cultures also kept fishes as pets in bowls or in ponds.

Freshwater Fishes

What is a freshwater fish? Fresh water describes water that does not have a lot of salt in it. Most lakes, rivers, streams, and ponds have fresh water. The fishes that live in those bodies of water are called freshwater fishes. The

As shown in this painting by Sir John Everett Millais, fishes have long been popular pets.

FISHES OR FISH?

In this book you will sometimes see the word *fishes,* but what does that mean? When you are reading about two or more fish that are the same **species,** or type, the word *fish* is used. When describing a group with many different species, *fishes* is used. For example, if you saw a tank with two mollies in it, you might say, "Look at those pretty fish." When you describe a tank with many mollies, guppies, and tetras, you should say, "Those fishes have very nice colors."

water in oceans and seas has a lot of salt in it. Fishes that live in those bodies of water are called saltwater fishes. They must have salt in the water or they will die.

Some freshwater and saltwater fishes can be kept as pets, but a fresh-water tank is easier to take care of. Saltwater tanks need more equipment and a lot more work. Saltwater fishes can also be more expensive than fresh-water fishes. Freshwater fishes are the best kind of fishes for a first-time fish owner. Today, freshwater fishes are the most popular pets in America. Many types of freshwater fishes are easy to care for and are fun to watch. So it is no surprise that one out of every ten pet owners has a pet fish.

2

Facts about Fishes

Freshwater fishes come in many sizes—from a tiny neon tetra to great big oscars. Long and slender or round and wide, fishes also come in many shapes. A fish's color is determined by the color of its **scales.** The scales are small plate-like pieces on the fish's skin. A fish has thousands of scales around its body. The scales are arranged together to form a sort of protective armor around the fish. The scale arrangement also determines the fish's color. Some fishes are one color, while others are a variety of colors. A layer of slime covers the scales. This slippery coating helps protect the fish. A fish without slime can get sick. This is one of the reasons why you should never pet your fish.

Though the bodies and sizes may be different, nearly all freshwater fishes have the same general features. Every fish has a tail. The color and shape of a fish's tail depends on the kind of fish it is. Fish tails can be flat and short, like the tail of a molly, or long and flowing, like the tail of a fancy goldfish, such as an oranda.

First-time fish keepers should start with freshwater fishes, such as these platys.

The scales are what give a fish its color. Some fish can be one color, while others—such as this calico-colored fantail goldfish—can be several different colors.

An oranda can be orange, white with a red patch on its head (this type of goldfish is called a redcap), or a chocolate color.

Fishes also have a number of fins. The dorsal fins are located on the fish's back. The two pectoral fins are located on the fish's sides. The pectoral fins usually stick out from the body, but can also move to lie flat against the fish's sides. Depending upon what kind of fish it is, a fish will also have one or more fins on the bottom side of its body—usually along its belly or near the tail. A fish moves around by using its fins and its tail. The pectoral fins move the water around the fish, so the fish can swim forward or

The sailfin mollie gets its name from the very tall dorsal fin across its back. This fin resembles a sail on a boat.

backward. The other fins and the tail also help keep the fish steady as it moves through the water.

A fish does not have a neck, so its head is part of its whole body. Nearly every fish has two eyes—one on each side of its head. Scientists believe that fish can see in color. Most fishes do not have eyelids, so they sleep with their eyes open.

A fish does not have a nose, but it does have two nostrils at the front of its face. Fishes are very sensitive to smells in the water, and use this sense

Black mollies are related to sailfin mollies, though they do not have the same very large dorsal fins. Black mollies are good fish for the first-time fish keeper.

These kissing gouramis are not kissing—they are actually fighting. They get their name from very large lips that look like they are puckering up for a kiss.

to locate food. Fishes have a sense of taste and may take small nibbles of food to taste it before eating. All fishes have mouths, but not all fishes have teeth. Fish without teeth do not chew their food. Instead, they swallow the food whole.

Breathing Underwater

Like all animals, fishes need air—specifically oxygen—to live. Many different animals—including humans—get oxygen by taking in air through their noses or mouths. The air goes through the lungs and is then used to keep the animal alive.

COLD-BLOODED

All fishes are cold-blooded. This does not mean that a fish's blood is always cold. Instead, it means that the fish is not able to control its own body temperature very well. A fish's body temperature will be about the same temperature as the water around it. This can be dangerous because if the water is too hot or too cold, the fish can get sick or die. Fish help to control their body temperatures by moving to warmer or colder areas. (This is similar to how reptiles, which are also cold-blooded, bask in the sun for heat, and move into the shade to cool down.) As a fish keeper, you will be responsible for keeping your fish's water just right.

Almost all fishes get their oxygen from the water around them. Water usually enters a fish's body through its mouth. The water then passes through the fish's **gills**. These structures are located on both sides of the fish's head. The gills take the oxygen out of the water so that the fish can breathe. If you watch a fish from the side, you can see its gills as it breathes. The gills will be a pink or red color.

There are some types of fishes that do not take oxygen from the water. Instead, they travel to the surface of the water and get oxygen from the air above. These fish are called **anabantoids** and have special structures inside their bodies that allow them to breathe air. Anabantoids that are kept as pets include bettas and gouramis.

3

Choosing Your Fish

There are hundreds of different types of freshwater fishes from which you can choose. Some of the most popular types of fishes, such as goldfish, catfish and guppies, can be found in your local pet store. Before you choose your fish, you should find out what different types of fishes need and how you should care for them. You should know how big the fish will be when it is full grown. All fish start out small, but some only grow to be two inches long, while others may be longer than eight inches! Also, if you plan on getting more than one fish, do some research and find out whether or not they will get along once you put them into the fish tank together. Here are some types of fishes that are good for people interested in pet fish.

Goldfish

Although there are more than one hundred types of goldfish, the goldfish that often make the best pets for first-time fish keepers are called comets.

Neon tetras—named for their bright colors—are very good fish for first-time fish keepers. They get along well with many other fishes.

Most pet stores have a wide variety of comets for sale.

Comets are the fish most commonly found at fairs and carnivals, though it is best to get your pet fish from a pet store. They can grow to be a few inches long and may live for several years.

You can keep your comet in a bowl instead of a fish tank as long as the bowl has a large opening at the top. When the surface of the water is exposed to the air, oxygen can make its way into the water so your goldfish can breathe. The bowl should be big enough for your fish to swim around easily. If you keep a comet in a fishbowl, you must be sure to change the fish's water at least once a week. Your fish will not be able to breathe in dirty water.

Some people prefer goldfish that are fancier than comets. These fancy goldfish are larger than comets and have brighter or bolder features. Unlike comets, however, fancy goldfish cannot be kept in a fishbowl. They must live in fish tanks that have equipment like **filters,** air pumps, and heaters.

One popular type of fancy goldfish is a fantail. Fantails have long, flowing tails and can come in many different colors. Orandas are another popular goldfish. Like fantails, orandas have long, flowing tails and fins, but their bodies are more round. Lionheads are another type of fancy goldfish. Their bodies are round with short tails and they do not have dorsal fins. A lionhead gets its name from the puffy growths around its head. Bubble eyes are an interesting-looking type of fancy goldfish. They have round bodies, long tails, but underneath each of their eyes is a bubble of skin, filled with water.

Bettas

There are more than fifty types of betta fish, but the most popular kind is the colorful Siamese fighting fish. You have probably seen these bettas displayed in small bowls in pet stores. A betta is a good fish for a first-time

This bubble-eye goldfish has pouches of water beneath its eyes. These are very delicate and can pop, which can make the fish sick.

fish keeper because it can be kept in a simple fish-bowl. Bettas can also be kept in a fish tank. Either way, you must make sure that the water is between 75 and 86 degrees Fahrenheit.

Bettas do not need a special air filter or air pump. They can take their oxygen directly from the air above the water.

Male bettas are very pretty, with bright colors and long, flowing fins and tails. Females are smaller, have shorter tails, and are not as brightly colored. Male bettas will fight other male or female bettas, so you should only have one male in a bowl or tank. However, you can have two or more female bettas together since they will not fight.

Mollies

Many fish keepers like raising mollies. These fish come in many different colors, such as orange, brown, and black. The black molly is a great fish for beginners because it is more peaceful than mollies of other colors. Either a male or a female molly makes a good pet, but if you have too many males

22

Koi

Koi (pronounced *koy*) are a type of carp, and are closely related to goldfish. Some varieties of koi even look like very big goldfish. Koi can grow to be one to two feet long, which is too large for a fish tank. This is why most koi are kept in backyard ponds. These ponds are specially made to hold these large fish, and contain hundreds of gallons of water. This is one reason why koi are not right for every fish keeper.

Like goldfish, they can have scales of many different and beautiful colors and patterns. In fact, many koi are displayed at special fish shows. Beautiful koi can be very expensive. Some prize-winning koi have even sold for more than ten thousand dollars!

and females together you might end up with a tank full of baby mollies. Mollies must be kept in fish tanks, and are comfortable in water that is between 70 and 82 degrees.

Guppies

Guppies are great starter fish for your tank because they get along will with all other fishes. Guppies are easier to take care of because they are not too sensitive to small changes in the water temperature and eat almost any kind of fish food. It is easy to tell male and female guppies apart because the male is usually more colorful, with a very beautiful tail. The female is usually larger with a thicker body and a smaller tail. Guppies grow to be about two inches long. Your guppies need to live in a fish tank with water that is between 66 and 84 degrees.

Gouramis

There are many types of gourami fish, but the dwarf gourami is the best gourami for beginners. The dwarf gourami is not only beautiful, but it can

Be careful when buying gouramis. Dwarf gouramis, such as these, get along with other fishes. Other types of gouramis, however, will fight and hurt other fishes in the tank.

be very easy to keep, as well. When full grown, a dwarf gourami will only be about two inches long. It is easy to tell a male and a female dwarf gourami apart because the male is more colorful than the female. The female dwarf gourami is usually gray or brown in appearance. Male dwarf gouramis can be blue or red. They are comfortable in water that is between 77 and 82 degrees.

If you decide to add a gourami to your tank, make sure you ask for a dwarf gourami. Other types of gouramis can grow to be up to ten inches long, and will fight with other fish.

Tetras

Tetras come in many varieties and are some of the most popular freshwater fishes kept as pets. Tetra colors range from deep blue and red, to silver and black. The neon-colored tetra is a good starter fish for your tank because it is very colorful and is a peaceful fish. Bleeding heart tetras are another type of tetra that gets along well with other fish. A bleeding heart gets its name from the red heart-shaped spot on its side. Other tetras, such as the red-eyed or black phantom tetras are not likely to get along with other types of fishes. Tetras swim in **schools** when there are two or more in an aquarium. They grow to be about two inches long and are most comfortable in water that is between 75 and 80 degrees.

25

Zebra Fish

Zebra fish are very fast swimmers and can be quite handsome. Most of their bodies are yellow or gold with four long blue or black stripes that run from the head to the tail. This makes the fish appear striped like a zebra. The top portion of the fish's body is brown and the belly area is pale yellow.

Zebra fish are good **community fish,** which means that they get along with other fishes. Zebra fish grow to be about two inches long and are most comfortable in water between 65 and 78 degrees.

Algae Eaters

Algae is a type of plant that grows in the water. If you have live plants in your tank or your tank is near a lot of sunlight, green or brown algae might grow on the walls or floor of the tank. Algae eaters are fish that eat this algae along with regular fish food.

There are several different types of fish that are considered algae eaters. Most have mouths that are shaped to scoop and suck up algae. (Some people think the fishes' mouths resemble suction cups.) Different types of algae eaters may grow to be anywhere from two inches to ten inches. For a small tank, you should make sure you buy an algae eater that will not grow too large.

Living Together

If you decide to have a bright and beautiful fish tank filled with many

Most algae eaters have long and slender bodies that can be a variety of colors. These fish can help keep a tank clean.

different kinds of fishes, you will have to think about how your new fishes will get along with each other. Some fishes are very peaceful and happy to live with or ignore other fishes in the tank. Other fishes will bite or attack their underwater neighbors. Aquarium fishes usually fall into three main categories—**nonaggressive, semi-aggressive,** and **aggressive.** People who work at the pet or fish stores will be able to give you advice on what fishes can be kept together.

Nonaggressive

Sometimes called a community fish, a nonaggressive fish is peaceful and gets along well with fish of its own species as well as other kinds of fishes.

A community tank has many different types of fishes that can get along. This tank has fantail guppies and gouramis living together peacefully.

In most cases, nonaggressive fishes will not fight with each other. Some peaceful fish include mollies, guppies, comets, zebra fish, and certain kinds of tetras.

Semi-Aggressive

These are fishes that get along with other types of fishes, but are likely to fight with other fish of the same species. You should only have one of each type of semi-aggressive fish in your fish tank. Some semi-aggressive fishes include angelfish, barbs, and freshwater sharks. The freshwater sharks that live in fish tanks, such as Bala or tri-colored sharks and rainbow sharks, are usually only a few inches long. These are not like the large sharks that swim in the oceans.

Aggressive

These fishes do not get along with other fishes. Aggressive fish will attack and sometimes eat other fish. An aggressive fish is usually kept in a tank with fish that belong to its species. In some cases, aggressive fish of the same species will fight with each other. The most popular aggressive fish is the Siamese fighting fish, or betta. You should not keep two males in a tank or bowl together because they will fight. However, it is okay to keep two or more females together in a fish tank. Other aggressive fish include oscars, different types of cichlids, and clown knife fish. One aggressive fish, the Jack Dempsey, was named after a boxer from the 1920s. In general, bettas are the only aggressive fish that first-time fish keepers should have. Aggressive fish usually require larger tanks and more care, which makes them better suited for experienced fish keepers.

Where to Buy

You can buy your fish from a large pet store or from stores that sell only (or mostly) fishes. Most pet stores have a large selection of fishes for sale. It is

Pet stores are the perfect place to buy your freshwater fishes. Most pet stores offer a variety of freshwater fishes, from small tetras to these large koi.

nice to have a big selection to choose from, but it is also good to buy your fish from people who seem to know a lot about fish. People who work in pet stores usually know about fishes and fish keeping. When choosing your fish, do not be afraid to ask questions. If the pet store worker knows a lot about fish, then you might feel better about the fish you are about to bring home. However, if you feel that the workers do not really know or care about the fish, you might be better off going to another store.

There are many things you should look for when buying your fish. Here are a few things to remember when searching for your fish.

- Is the water in the different tanks clear or cloudy?
- Do the fish look healthy? Are any fish in the tank swimming upside down?
- Do any of the fish have strange bumps on their bodies? Do they have any white spots or fuzzy blobs on their scales? (These growths are a sign of sickness.)
- Are there dead fish in the tank? (Dead fish can mean that there is some sort of illness in the tank.)
- When looking closely at the fish you want, do you notice any problems with its body? Does it have all of its fins? Is the tail complete and not ragged or broken?
- Do the fish seem active? If they are nonaggressive community fish, are they swimming alongside other fish?

You should not buy fish that live in a tank with any sign of illness. Even if the fish you choose looks healthy, it could still be sick. Do not be afraid to ask questions about the fish you want to buy. You definitely want your new fish friend to be healthy.

4

Caring for Your Fish

Before you bring your fish home, you need to set up its new home. Whether you will keep it in a bowl or tank, you must have everything ready before you get your fish. All the supplies you will need to keep a fish are available at your local pet stores. What you need depends on the type and number of fish you will be keeping.

Your Fish's Home

If you have a small fish that can live in a bowl, such as a comet or a betta, then your job is a lot easier. You just need to pick out a bowl that is big enough to hold your fish. You should also make sure that it is not too hard to clean. Fishbowls can be made of glass or plastic.

Fancy goldfish and most other fishes will need fish tanks with more equipment. Fish tanks come in all sizes and shapes. Tanks can be made out of plastic or glass. Plastic fish tanks are not as heavy as glass tanks and many

With the proper supplies, hard work, and patience, you can have a tank full of happy and healthy fishes.

pet owners think that the plastic walls stay cleaner than glass walls. Most larger tanks are made of glass.

Tanks are measured by how many gallons of water they can hold. For example, tanks for freshwater fish can be anywhere from two gallons to one hundred gallons or more! The size you choose depends on many things. If you plan on having large fishes or many fishes, you will

Sometimes it can be hard to set up a fish tank. You should always have the help of an adult before you set up the tank.

need a bigger tank. A good general rule is to allow one gallon of water for every fish in the tank. (For small fish like guppies, you will probably be able to fit more than two guppies in a two-gallon tank.) Putting too many fish in one tank will crowd your fish. The fish will not have enough room to swim around, and the tank will get dirty very easily. A five-gallon tank is a good size for beginners. A fish tank this size can provide a comfortable home for about four fish.

Artificial plants and other decorations can help to make your aquarium more lively.

Sometimes, a fish will jump out of the tank or things will fall into the water. Putting a cover on the tank is one way to prevent these things from happening. Pet stores sell tank covers in many different sizes. These covers are usually made of plastic, and fit right on top of the tank. It is better to buy a ready-made cover instead of using something you have around the house. The ready-made covers allow light to pass into to the tank. Also, the covers are not too heavy and will not break your tank.

Some tank covers come with built-in lights. These lights use special bulbs and need to be plugged into an electrical outlet. The lights will make it easier for you to see your fish. The lights will also let your fish know what time of day it is. Fish do sleep, so be sure to turn the light off at night.

You do not have to have a special light built into the tank cover. Some people just position lamps near the tank. These lamps can provide enough light for the fish, but you must be very careful. Lights built into a tank cover are specially made so that the water from the tank will not destroy the lights or cause an electrical fire. Regular lamps kept near water can be a very dangerous fire hazard. You should discuss this with an adult before you set up your tank.

Some people keep their tanks near a window for light. You can do this, but there might be problems. Too much sunlight can make your fish's water too hot. Too much sunlight can also cause algae to grow in your tank. During cooler months, putting a tank near a drafty window may make your fish's water too cold. These are just some things you should consider when setting up your tank.

Filters, Air Pumps, and Heaters

The purpose of a filter is to remove extra food, dangerous chemicals, and the fish's waste products from the water. The filter needs electricity to run, so it must be plugged into an outlet. There are many types of filters. The most common type of filter usually hangs on the back of the tank. A hard plastic tube runs from the filter box into the tank. The filter sucks in water through the tube, cleans it, and then puts the clean water back into the tank. Larger tanks need stronger filters. You can check with your local pet store to find out what size filter you should buy. Some tanks are sold with filters.

Air pumps or aerators blow air into the tank water. It helps to provide

...ir pumps, heaters, and tank filters come in a variety of shapes ...nd sizes.

your fish with the oxygen it needs to breathe. Like filters, air pumps have little motors that need electricity to run. The air pump is usually a small square or rectangular box that sits next to or beneath your fish tank. A flexible tube goes from the pump into the tank. When the pump is working, air bubbles will come out of the tube and into the water.

Your fish's health depends on how cold or warm its water is. Different types of fishes like different water temperatures. You can monitor the water temperature by using special tank thermometers. Some tank thermometers go inside the tank. Made of glass or plastic, they attach to the side of the tank with suction cups. Pet stores also sell special thermometer strips. These strips are stuck to the outside of the tank and change color as the water temperature changes. Always use a thermometer that is made specifically for fish tanks.

Heaters are used to keep aquarium water warm. The heater always stays plugged into an electrical outlet. If the water gets too cold, the heater will turn on and warm the water. You should only use a special aquarium

All objects that are going into the tank, such as gravel, plants, or decorations, must be carefully washed.

heater to keep your tank water at the right temperature. Never use a portable household heater (also called space heaters) to heat your tank from the outside. Those kinds of heaters cannot keep all of the tank water warm enough. They can also melt and destroy your tank, and can cause a fire in your home.

Gravel and Decorations

You do not have to have gravel or decorations in your tank. Your fish can be happy without them. If you do want gravel and decorations, you will have to put in a little more work. Tanks with gravel are harder to clean than tanks without gravel. However, many feel that an attractive tank with active fish and colorful gravel and decorations is worth the extra effort.

You should always buy the gravel and decorations from a pet store.

Objects from your backyard might be harmful to the fish because dirt, bugs, mold, and other things will make the water dirty and could even make your fish sick. Gravel comes in many sizes and colors. Labels on the bags of gravel sold at pet stores will tell you how much gravel you will need for different-size tanks.

You might also want to get other decorations, such fake wood or plants to provide a natural environment for your fish. Plastic plants and wood can look very natural in a fish tank and will not make the water dirty, the way real plants and wood can. Some fish might also eat the live plants or nibble on the real wood, which could make them sick. Most pet stores sell plenty of decorations that will be safe for your fish and will make your fish tank look beautiful.

Putting It All Together

Setting up a fish tank can be hard work, so ask an adult to help you. Start preparing your fish tank a few days before you start adding fish to the water. Rinse out your fish tank in the tub or outside with a hose. Some people add a little table salt to help clean out the tank. If you do this, however, you must make sure you rinse the tank very well so that all the salt is gone. Never use soap or detergent to clean the tank or anything that goes into the tank. It can be hard to rinse off all of the soap. Any soap in the tank or water will make your fish sick.

You must wash any decorations that are going into your tank. Use hot water to rinse the plastic plants, fake wood, or other decorations. If you plan on putting gravel in your tank, you must wash the gravel first. Pour the gravel into a bucket or large bowl. Add water to the bowl or bucket until the gravel is covered. Use your hand to mix around the gravel. (This should make the water cloudy.) Carefully pour out the water, making sure none of the gravel falls out. Add clean water to the bucket or bowl, swish around the gravel, and dump the water. Repeat this until the water is clear.

Put your fish tank on a strong table that does not wobble when you try to move it. Pet stores also sell special tank stands made to hold fish tanks. These can be wooden or metal. If you have a tank light, filter, air pump, or heater, you need to keep your tank near an electrical outlet. Make sure the table or tank stand is near an electrical outlet.

Add the gravel to the tank until it is about one or two inches deep. You can also add other decorations to the tank, such as stones or other decorations. To add the plants, dig a small hole in the gravel, place the plant in the hole and then push the gravel back around the plant. You can position decorations this way, too.

The filter and air pump come with instructions. With an adult's help, follow the instructions to set up the filter and air pump. Place the heater and thermometer in the tank. Do not plug in the filter, pump, or heater until the tank is filled with water.

Slowly add water to your tank until the tank is filled. The safest way to do this is to keep your tank on the stand or table and add water with a bucket. This way the tank will not be too heavy to carry and you will not risk dropping it. Be sure to add the water slowly, so you do not move the gravel around when you pour the water.

Put the cover back on the tank. Plug in the filter, pump, and heater and turn them on. The filter, heater, and pump should be plugged in and running at all times. Make sure that the plugs and electrical outlets you use do not get wet. Check on your tank in a few hours to make sure the temperature is right and that the air pump and filter are working. In a few days your tank will be ready for your new fish.

Adding Fish to Your Tank

You will need an adult's help when adding your fish to the tank or bowl. Your new fish will come home in a bag with water and air. Do not immediately pour the fish into the tank or bowl. Carefully rinse the outside of the bag to make sure that no dirt is stuck to it. Add some of the tank water to the bag. Tie the bag and gently place it in the tank or bowl. Allow the bag to float around the tank for about twenty minutes. This will bring the temperature of the water in the bag close to the temperature of the water in the tank. This helps your fish adjust to its new tank.

Carefully open the bag and use a small net to move the fish from

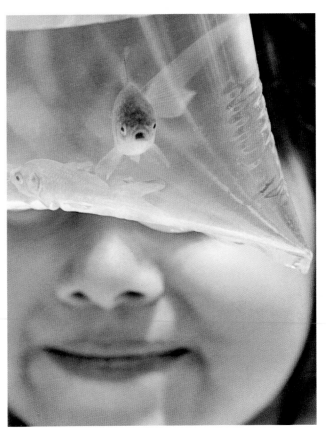

Your fish will come home from the pet store in a plastic bag with water and air.

the bag to the tank. Do not pour in the water from the bag. (After the fish is out, you can dump the bag water down a tub drain, in the toilet, or outside.) Your fish may be nervous at first, so give it time to adjust. In a few hours your fish will most likely be swimming around, happy in its new home.

Keeping Your Fish Healthy

With proper care, your pet fish can live for many years. In order to keep it healthy, you must feed it regularly and keep the tank or bowl clean. You should check the water temperature every day. If the water is too hot or too

Pet stores can give you advice on what you should feed your fish and how often. Feeding the fish too much will dirty your tank and make your fish sick.

cold, ask an adult to help you adjust the tank heater. You will also need to make sure the heater, filter, light and air pump are running. The light can be turned off for twelve hours at night (so the fish can sleep), but the heater, filter and pump should be running all of the time.

Feeding

Different types of fish need different types of food. Some fish prefer small flakes, while others need pellets or other forms of food. Your local pet store sells many different kinds of food. The labels on the food will tell you what kind of food to feed and how much. You can also ask someone who works at the pet store. Even though you may think your fish looks hungry, you should only feed what the label or pet store worker recommends. Extra food in the tank will make the water dirty. This makes it hard for your fish to breathe and may make it sick. Never feed your fish human food. This can poison your fish and make the water very dirty.

Cleaning

How often you clean the tank or bowl depends on many things. If you have a bowl, you will need to change the water about once a week. You might need to change the water more often if the bowl gets very dirty quickly. Carefully move your fish into another container. You must make sure this container has some of the water from the bowl. (Never put your fish into a bowl or tank that is filled with brand-new water.) Empty your bowl out and wash it with hot water. Refill the bowl and make sure the water is the right temperature. Put the fish and the water it is in back into the bowl.

If you have a very strong filter, you will not have to clean the tank as often. But if you have many fish that eat a lot, the water will get dirty faster. A dirty tank will make your fish sick. Also, dirty tank water smells really bad and can be unhealthy for humans, too.

In most cases, you should never change all of the water in a fish tank. This can harm your fish. But it is important that you clean out the fish waste and dirty water. Exchanging some of the dirty water for clean water is called a partial water change. Most fish keepers recommend cleaning the tank and doing a partial water change at least twice a month.

The easiest way to change part of the water and get rid of some of the fish waste is to use a **siphon** and a bucket. Have an adult help you use the siphon. (Instructions usually come with siphons, or you can ask someone at a pet store to explain how to use one.) The siphon will suck up dirt and dirty water and drain it into a nearby bucket. When the bucket is almost

WARNING!

Fish water—clean or dirty—can carry germs or other organisms that can make humans sick. Never clean a fishbowl or tank in your kitchen or bathroom sink. You do not want to put fish wastes anywhere near where you wash your dishes, get drinking water, or brush your teeth.

Dirty fish water should be dumped down a tub drain, down the toilet, or outside. If you pour the dirty water into the tub or toilet, be sure to have an adult help you clean the tub or toilet afterward. Cleaning your fish's water keeps it healthy, but you also want to make sure you stay healthy, too!

A tank that is set up properly and filled with healthy fishes can bring years of joy to many fish keepers.

full, pull the siphon out of the water. Get rid of the dirty water and start siphoning again. Because the fish will stay in the tank while you are cleaning it, you should leave about half of the water in the tank at all times.

When you have removed about half of the water, stop siphoning. Rinse the bucket out and add clean tap water. Make sure the water in the bucket is close to the temperature of the water in the tank. Slowly pour the water into the tank. Keep adding water until the tank is full. You will also need to keep your filter clean. Follow the filter's instructions on how to clean it.

With careful care and attention, freshwater fishes can make perfect pets. Healthy fish can bring you many years of fun and excitement as a happy and proud fish keeper.

Glossary

algae—A brown or green plant that can grow on surfaces in fish tanks or fishbowls.

aggressive—Likely to fight or attack other fishes.

anabantoids—A type of fish that takes oxygen from the air.

carp—A type of fish. People have raised and kept carp for food or as pets for thousands of years.

community fish—A fish that can live peacefully with other fishes—also called nonaggressive fish.

filter—A piece of aquarium equipment that helps keep a fish tank clean.

nonaggressive—Not likely to attack or fight with other fish. Nonaggressive fish are often called community fish.

oxygen—An element (in air or water) that all animals need in order to live.

scales—Small, thin, flat, plates that protect a fish's body.

schools—Groups of fish that swim together.

semi-aggressive—Likely to attack or fight with fish of the same species, but able to live peacefully with different species of fishes.

siphon—One of the tools needed to clean out the aquarium. A siphon hose is a long, hollow tube that sucks water and dirt out of the tank and into a bucket.

species—A particular type of plant or animal.

Find Out More

Books

Barnes, Julia. *101 Facts about Goldfish*. Milwaukee, WI: Gareth Stevens, 2002.

Hamilton, Lynn. *Caring for Your Fish*. Mankato, MN: Weigl, 2003.

MacAulay, Kelley and Bobbie Kalman. *Goldfish*. New York: Crabtree Pub. Co., 2004.

Schliewen, Ulrich. *Tropical Freshwater Aquarium Fish from A to Z*. Hauppauge, NY: Barron's Educational Series, 2005.

Silverstein, Alvin and Virginia Silverstein. *Fabulous Fish*. Brookfield, CT: Twenty-First Century Books, 2003.

Web Sites

Fish Care from ASPCA's ANIMALAND
http://www.aspca.org/site/PageServer?pagename=kids_pc_fish_411

Fish as Pets
http://library.thinkquest.org/J003021/fish.html

There's Something Fishy Going on
http://www.fishedz.com

Index

About the Author

Marjorie L. Buckmaster lives in New Jersey with her daughter. They have eight pets, including a dog, three cats, two rabbits, and two goldfish.